MAINTENANCE REQUEST F

OWNER INFORMATION

COMPANY	
TELEPHONE	
ADDRESS	
EMAIL	

FORM INFORMATION

Start Date:	End Date:

Enjoying this book?
You can recommend this book to others by leaving a review on our page. We would love to know your thoughts on how you use our books. **IT MEANS A LOT TO US**

Thank you for your support. You are awesome!

IF FOUND, PLEASE CONTACT	OR

Company's copy

REQUEST NO:	DATE OF REQUEST:	REQUEST BY:

LOCATION:	TELEPHONE:

PROBLEM:

PRIORITY URGENT ◯ NOT URGENT ◯ NOT VERY URGENT ◯

ASSIGNED TO:	DATE STARTED:	DATE COMPLETED:

TOTAL TIME SPENT:	TOTAL COST:

COMMENT:

✂ -

REQUEST NO:	DATE OF REQUEST:	REQUEST BY:

LOCATION:	TELEPHONE:

PROBLEM:

PRIORITY URGENT ◯ NOT URGENT ◯ NOT VERY URGENT ◯

ASSIGNED TO:	DATE STARTED:	DATE COMPLETED:

TOTAL TIME SPENT:	TOTAL COST:

COMMENT:

Company's copy

REQUEST NO:	DATE OF REQUEST:	REQUEST BY:

LOCATION:	TELEPHONE:

PROBLEM:

PRIORITY URGENT ◯ NOT URGENT ◯ NOT VERY URGENT ◯

ASSIGNED TO:	DATE STARTED:	DATE COMPLETED:

TOTAL TIME SPENT:	TOTAL COST:

COMMENT:

- ✂

REQUEST NO:	DATE OF REQUEST:	REQUEST BY:

LOCATION:	TELEPHONE:

PROBLEM:

PRIORITY URGENT ◯ NOT URGENT ◯ NOT VERY URGENT ◯

ASSIGNED TO:	DATE STARTED:	DATE COMPLETED:

TOTAL TIME SPENT:	TOTAL COST:

COMMENT:

Company's copy

REQUEST NO:	DATE OF REQUEST:	REQUEST BY:

LOCATION:	TELEPHONE:

PROBLEM:

PRIORITY URGENT ◯ NOT URGENT ◯ NOT VERY URGENT ◯

ASSIGNED TO:	DATE STARTED:	DATE COMPLETED:

TOTAL TIME SPENT:	TOTAL COST:

COMMENT:

- ✂

REQUEST NO:	DATE OF REQUEST:	REQUEST BY:

LOCATION:	TELEPHONE:

PROBLEM:

PRIORITY URGENT ◯ NOT URGENT ◯ NOT VERY URGENT ◯

ASSIGNED TO:	DATE STARTED:	DATE COMPLETED:

TOTAL TIME SPENT:	TOTAL COST:

COMMENT:

Company's copy

REQUEST NO:	DATE OF REQUEST:	REQUEST BY:

LOCATION:	TELEPHONE:

PROBLEM:

PRIORITY URGENT ◯ NOT URGENT ◯ NOT VERY URGENT ◯

ASSIGNED TO:	DATE STARTED:	DATE COMPLETED:

TOTAL TIME SPENT:	TOTAL COST:

COMMENT:

- ✂

REQUEST NO:	DATE OF REQUEST:	REQUEST BY:

LOCATION:	TELEPHONE:

PROBLEM:

PRIORITY URGENT ◯ NOT URGENT ◯ NOT VERY URGENT ◯

ASSIGNED TO:	DATE STARTED:	DATE COMPLETED:

TOTAL TIME SPENT:	TOTAL COST:

COMMENT:

Company's copy

REQUEST NO:	DATE OF REQUEST:	REQUEST BY:

LOCATION:	TELEPHONE:

PROBLEM:

PRIORITY URGENT ⚪ NOT URGENT ⚪ NOT VERY URGENT ⚪

ASSIGNED TO:	DATE STARTED:	DATE COMPLETED:

TOTAL TIME SPENT:	TOTAL COST:

COMMENT:

--- ✂

REQUEST NO:	DATE OF REQUEST:	REQUEST BY:

LOCATION:	TELEPHONE:

PROBLEM:

PRIORITY URGENT ⚪ NOT URGENT ⚪ NOT VERY URGENT ⚪

ASSIGNED TO:	DATE STARTED:	DATE COMPLETED:

TOTAL TIME SPENT:	TOTAL COST:

COMMENT:

Company's copy

MAINTENANCE REQUEST FORM

REQUEST NO:	DATE OF REQUEST:	REQUEST BY:

LOCATION:	TELEPHONE:

PROBLEM:

PRIORITY   URGENT ◯   NOT URGENT ◯   NOT VERY URGENT ◯

ASSIGNED TO:	DATE STARTED:	DATE COMPLETED:

TOTAL TIME SPENT:	TOTAL COST:

COMMENT:

- ✂

REQUEST NO:	DATE OF REQUEST:	REQUEST BY:

LOCATION:	TELEPHONE:

PROBLEM:

PRIORITY   URGENT ◯   NOT URGENT ◯   NOT VERY URGENT ◯

ASSIGNED TO:	DATE STARTED:	DATE COMPLETED:

TOTAL TIME SPENT:	TOTAL COST:

COMMENT:

Company's copy

REQUEST NO:	DATE OF REQUEST:	REQUEST BY:

LOCATION:	TELEPHONE:

PROBLEM:

PRIORITY URGENT ◯ NOT URGENT ◯ NOT VERY URGENT◯

ASSIGNED TO:	DATE STARTED:	DATE COMPLETED:

TOTAL TIME SPENT:	TOTAL COST:

COMMENT:

- ✂

REQUEST NO:	DATE OF REQUEST:	REQUEST BY:

LOCATION:	TELEPHONE:

PROBLEM:

PRIORITY URGENT ◯ NOT URGENT ◯ NOT VERY URGENT◯

ASSIGNED TO:	DATE STARTED:	DATE COMPLETED:

TOTAL TIME SPENT:	TOTAL COST:

COMMENT:

Company's copy

REQUEST NO:	DATE OF REQUEST:	REQUEST BY:

LOCATION:	TELEPHONE:

PROBLEM:

PRIORITY   URGENT ◯   NOT URGENT ◯   NOT VERY URGENT ◯

ASSIGNED TO:	DATE STARTED:	DATE COMPLETED:

TOTAL TIME SPENT:	TOTAL COST:

COMMENT:

- ✂

REQUEST NO:	DATE OF REQUEST:	REQUEST BY:

LOCATION:	TELEPHONE:

PROBLEM:

PRIORITY   URGENT ◯   NOT URGENT ◯   NOT VERY URGENT ◯

ASSIGNED TO:	DATE STARTED:	DATE COMPLETED:

TOTAL TIME SPENT:	TOTAL COST:

COMMENT:

Company's copy

REQUEST NO:	DATE OF REQUEST:	REQUEST BY:

LOCATION:	TELEPHONE:

PROBLEM:

PRIORITY URGENT ⚪ NOT URGENT ⚪ NOT VERY URGENT ⚪

ASSIGNED TO:	DATE STARTED:	DATE COMPLETED:

TOTAL TIME SPENT:	TOTAL COST:

COMMENT:

- ✂

REQUEST NO:	DATE OF REQUEST:	REQUEST BY:

LOCATION:	TELEPHONE:

PROBLEM:

PRIORITY URGENT ⚪ NOT URGENT ⚪ NOT VERY URGENT ⚪

ASSIGNED TO:	DATE STARTED:	DATE COMPLETED:

TOTAL TIME SPENT:	TOTAL COST:

COMMENT:

19

Company's copy

REQUEST NO:	DATE OF REQUEST:	REQUEST BY:

LOCATION:	TELEPHONE:

PROBLEM:

PRIORITY URGENT ⬤ NOT URGENT ⬤ NOT VERY URGENT ⬤

ASSIGNED TO:	DATE STARTED:	DATE COMPLETED:

TOTAL TIME SPENT:	TOTAL COST:

COMMENT:

--✂

REQUEST NO:	DATE OF REQUEST:	REQUEST BY:

LOCATION:	TELEPHONE:

PROBLEM:

PRIORITY URGENT ⬤ NOT URGENT ⬤ NOT VERY URGENT ⬤

ASSIGNED TO:	DATE STARTED:	DATE COMPLETED:

TOTAL TIME SPENT:	TOTAL COST:

COMMENT:

Company's copy

REQUEST NO:	DATE OF REQUEST:	REQUEST BY:

LOCATION:	TELEPHONE:

PROBLEM:

PRIORITY   URGENT ◯   NOT URGENT ◯   NOT VERY URGENT ◯

ASSIGNED TO:	DATE STARTED:	DATE COMPLETED:

TOTAL TIME SPENT:	TOTAL COST:

COMMENT:

✂ · ✂

REQUEST NO:	DATE OF REQUEST:	REQUEST BY:

LOCATION:	TELEPHONE:

PROBLEM:

PRIORITY   URGENT ◯   NOT URGENT ◯   NOT VERY URGENT ◯

ASSIGNED TO:	DATE STARTED:	DATE COMPLETED:

TOTAL TIME SPENT:	TOTAL COST:

COMMENT:

Company's copy

REQUEST NO:	DATE OF REQUEST:	REQUEST BY:

LOCATION:	TELEPHONE:

PROBLEM:

PRIORITY   URGENT ◯   NOT URGENT ◯   NOT VERY URGENT ◯

ASSIGNED TO:	DATE STARTED:	DATE COMPLETED:

TOTAL TIME SPENT:	TOTAL COST:

COMMENT:

- ✂

REQUEST NO:	DATE OF REQUEST:	REQUEST BY:

LOCATION:	TELEPHONE:

PROBLEM:

PRIORITY   URGENT ◯   NOT URGENT ◯   NOT VERY URGENT ◯

ASSIGNED TO:	DATE STARTED:	DATE COMPLETED:

TOTAL TIME SPENT:	TOTAL COST:

COMMENT:

Company's copy

REQUEST NO:	DATE OF REQUEST:	REQUEST BY:

LOCATION:	TELEPHONE:

PROBLEM:

PRIORITY URGENT ◯ NOT URGENT ◯ NOT VERY URGENT ◯

ASSIGNED TO:	DATE STARTED:	DATE COMPLETED:

TOTAL TIME SPENT:	TOTAL COST:

COMMENT:

- ✂

REQUEST NO:	DATE OF REQUEST:	REQUEST BY:

LOCATION:	TELEPHONE:

PROBLEM:

PRIORITY URGENT ◯ NOT URGENT ◯ NOT VERY URGENT ◯

ASSIGNED TO:	DATE STARTED:	DATE COMPLETED:

TOTAL TIME SPENT:	TOTAL COST:

COMMENT:

MAINTENANCE REQUEST FORM

REQUEST NO:	DATE OF REQUEST:	REQUEST BY:

LOCATION:	TELEPHONE:

PROBLEM:

PRIORITY	URGENT ⚪	NOT URGENT ⚪	NOT VERY URGENT ⚪

ASSIGNED TO:	DATE STARTED:	DATE COMPLETED:

TOTAL TIME SPENT:	TOTAL COST:

COMMENT:

- ✂

REQUEST NO:	DATE OF REQUEST:	REQUEST BY:

LOCATION:	TELEPHONE:

PROBLEM:

PRIORITY	URGENT ⚪	NOT URGENT ⚪	NOT VERY URGENT ⚪

ASSIGNED TO:	DATE STARTED:	DATE COMPLETED:

TOTAL TIME SPENT:	TOTAL COST:

COMMENT:

29

MAINTENANCE REQUEST FORM

REQUEST NO:	DATE OF REQUEST:	REQUEST BY:

LOCATION:	TELEPHONE:

PROBLEM:

PRIORITY URGENT ◯ NOT URGENT ◯ NOT VERY URGENT ◯

ASSIGNED TO:	DATE STARTED:	DATE COMPLETED:

TOTAL TIME SPENT:	TOTAL COST:

COMMENT:

- ✂

REQUEST NO:	DATE OF REQUEST:	REQUEST BY:

LOCATION:	TELEPHONE:

PROBLEM:

PRIORITY URGENT ◯ NOT URGENT ◯ NOT VERY URGENT ◯

ASSIGNED TO:	DATE STARTED:	DATE COMPLETED:

TOTAL TIME SPENT:	TOTAL COST:

COMMENT:

Company's copy

REQUEST NO:	DATE OF REQUEST:	REQUEST BY:

LOCATION:	TELEPHONE:

PROBLEM:

PRIORITY URGENT ◯ NOT URGENT ◯ NOT VERY URGENT ◯

ASSIGNED TO:	DATE STARTED:	DATE COMPLETED:

TOTAL TIME SPENT:	TOTAL COST:

COMMENT:

---- ✂ ----

REQUEST NO:	DATE OF REQUEST:	REQUEST BY:

LOCATION:	TELEPHONE:

PROBLEM:

PRIORITY URGENT ◯ NOT URGENT ◯ NOT VERY URGENT ◯

ASSIGNED TO:	DATE STARTED:	DATE COMPLETED:

TOTAL TIME SPENT:	TOTAL COST:

COMMENT:

Company's copy

REQUEST NO:	DATE OF REQUEST:	REQUEST BY:

LOCATION:	TELEPHONE:

PROBLEM:

PRIORITY   URGENT ◯   NOT URGENT ◯   NOT VERY URGENT ◯

ASSIGNED TO:	DATE STARTED:	DATE COMPLETED:

TOTAL TIME SPENT:	TOTAL COST:

COMMENT:

- ✂

REQUEST NO:	DATE OF REQUEST:	REQUEST BY:

LOCATION:	TELEPHONE:

PROBLEM:

PRIORITY   URGENT ◯   NOT URGENT ◯   NOT VERY URGENT ◯

ASSIGNED TO:	DATE STARTED:	DATE COMPLETED:

TOTAL TIME SPENT:	TOTAL COST:

COMMENT:

Company's copy

REQUEST NO:	DATE OF REQUEST:	REQUEST BY:

LOCATION:	TELEPHONE:

PROBLEM:

PRIORITY   URGENT ◯   NOT URGENT ◯   NOT VERY URGENT ◯

ASSIGNED TO:	DATE STARTED:	DATE COMPLETED:

TOTAL TIME SPENT:	TOTAL COST:

COMMENT:

- ✂

REQUEST NO:	DATE OF REQUEST:	REQUEST BY:

LOCATION:	TELEPHONE:

PROBLEM:

PRIORITY   URGENT ◯   NOT URGENT ◯   NOT VERY URGENT ◯

ASSIGNED TO:	DATE STARTED:	DATE COMPLETED:

TOTAL TIME SPENT:	TOTAL COST:

COMMENT:

Company's copy

REQUEST NO:	DATE OF REQUEST:	REQUEST BY:

LOCATION:	TELEPHONE:

PROBLEM:

PRIORITY   URGENT ◯   NOT URGENT ◯   NOT VERY URGENT ◯

ASSIGNED TO:	DATE STARTED:	DATE COMPLETED:

TOTAL TIME SPENT:	TOTAL COST:

COMMENT:

- ✂

REQUEST NO:	DATE OF REQUEST:	REQUEST BY:

LOCATION:	TELEPHONE:

PROBLEM:

PRIORITY   URGENT ◯   NOT URGENT ◯   NOT VERY URGENT ◯

ASSIGNED TO:	DATE STARTED:	DATE COMPLETED:

TOTAL TIME SPENT:	TOTAL COST:

COMMENT:

Company's copy

REQUEST NO:	DATE OF REQUEST:	REQUEST BY:

LOCATION:	TELEPHONE:

PROBLEM:

PRIORITY URGENT ◯ NOT URGENT ◯ NOT VERY URGENT ◯

ASSIGNED TO:	DATE STARTED:	DATE COMPLETED:

TOTAL TIME SPENT:	TOTAL COST:

COMMENT:

- ✂

REQUEST NO:	DATE OF REQUEST:	REQUEST BY:

LOCATION:	TELEPHONE:

PROBLEM:

PRIORITY URGENT ◯ NOT URGENT ◯ NOT VERY URGENT ◯

ASSIGNED TO:	DATE STARTED:	DATE COMPLETED:

TOTAL TIME SPENT:	TOTAL COST:

COMMENT:

Company's copy

REQUEST NO:	DATE OF REQUEST:	REQUEST BY:

LOCATION:	TELEPHONE:

PROBLEM:

PRIORITY   URGENT ◯   NOT URGENT ◯   NOT VERY URGENT ◯

ASSIGNED TO:	DATE STARTED:	DATE COMPLETED:

TOTAL TIME SPENT:	TOTAL COST:

COMMENT:

- ✂

REQUEST NO:	DATE OF REQUEST:	REQUEST BY:

LOCATION:	TELEPHONE:

PROBLEM:

PRIORITY   URGENT ◯   NOT URGENT ◯   NOT VERY URGENT ◯

ASSIGNED TO:	DATE STARTED:	DATE COMPLETED:

TOTAL TIME SPENT:	TOTAL COST:

COMMENT:

Company's copy

REQUEST NO:	DATE OF REQUEST:	REQUEST BY:

LOCATION:	TELEPHONE:

PROBLEM:

PRIORITY URGENT ○ NOT URGENT ○ NOT VERY URGENT ○

ASSIGNED TO:	DATE STARTED:	DATE COMPLETED:

TOTAL TIME SPENT:	TOTAL COST:

COMMENT:

- ✂

REQUEST NO:	DATE OF REQUEST:	REQUEST BY:

LOCATION:	TELEPHONE:

PROBLEM:

PRIORITY URGENT ○ NOT URGENT ○ NOT VERY URGENT ○

ASSIGNED TO:	DATE STARTED:	DATE COMPLETED:

TOTAL TIME SPENT:	TOTAL COST:

COMMENT:

Company's copy

REQUEST NO:	DATE OF REQUEST:	REQUEST BY:

LOCATION:	TELEPHONE:

PROBLEM:

PRIORITY URGENT ◯ NOT URGENT ◯ NOT VERY URGENT ◯

ASSIGNED TO:	DATE STARTED:	DATE COMPLETED:

TOTAL TIME SPENT:	TOTAL COST:

COMMENT:

- ✂

REQUEST NO:	DATE OF REQUEST:	REQUEST BY:

LOCATION:	TELEPHONE:

PROBLEM:

PRIORITY URGENT ◯ NOT URGENT ◯ NOT VERY URGENT ◯

ASSIGNED TO:	DATE STARTED:	DATE COMPLETED:

TOTAL TIME SPENT:	TOTAL COST:

COMMENT:

Company's copy

REQUEST NO: | DATE OF REQUEST: | REQUEST BY:

LOCATION: | TELEPHONE:

PROBLEM:

PRIORITY URGENT ◯ NOT URGENT ◯ NOT VERY URGENT ◯

ASSIGNED TO: | DATE STARTED: | DATE COMPLETED:

TOTAL TIME SPENT: | TOTAL COST:

COMMENT:

✂- -

REQUEST NO: | DATE OF REQUEST: | REQUEST BY:

LOCATION: | TELEPHONE:

PROBLEM:

PRIORITY URGENT ◯ NOT URGENT ◯ NOT VERY URGENT ◯

ASSIGNED TO: | DATE STARTED: | DATE COMPLETED:

TOTAL TIME SPENT: | TOTAL COST:

COMMENT:

MAINTENANCE REQUEST FORM

REQUEST NO:	DATE OF REQUEST:	REQUEST BY:

LOCATION:	TELEPHONE:

PROBLEM:

PRIORITY URGENT ◯ NOT URGENT ◯ NOT VERY URGENT ◯

ASSIGNED TO:	DATE STARTED:	DATE COMPLETED:

TOTAL TIME SPENT:	TOTAL COST:

COMMENT:

- ✂

REQUEST NO:	DATE OF REQUEST:	REQUEST BY:

LOCATION:	TELEPHONE:

PROBLEM:

PRIORITY URGENT ◯ NOT URGENT ◯ NOT VERY URGENT ◯

ASSIGNED TO:	DATE STARTED:	DATE COMPLETED:

TOTAL TIME SPENT:	TOTAL COST:

COMMENT:

Company's copy

REQUEST NO:	DATE OF REQUEST:	REQUEST BY:

LOCATION:	TELEPHONE:

PROBLEM:

PRIORITY URGENT ◯ NOT URGENT ◯ NOT VERY URGENT ◯

ASSIGNED TO:	DATE STARTED:	DATE COMPLETED:

TOTAL TIME SPENT:	TOTAL COST:

COMMENT:

- ✂

REQUEST NO:	DATE OF REQUEST:	REQUEST BY:

LOCATION:	TELEPHONE:

PROBLEM:

PRIORITY URGENT ◯ NOT URGENT ◯ NOT VERY URGENT ◯

ASSIGNED TO:	DATE STARTED:	DATE COMPLETED:

TOTAL TIME SPENT:	TOTAL COST:

COMMENT:

Company's copy

REQUEST NO:	DATE OF REQUEST:	REQUEST BY:

LOCATION:	TELEPHONE:

PROBLEM:

PRIORITY URGENT ◯ NOT URGENT ◯ NOT VERY URGENT ◯

ASSIGNED TO:	DATE STARTED:	DATE COMPLETED:

TOTAL TIME SPENT:	TOTAL COST:

COMMENT:

- ✂

REQUEST NO:	DATE OF REQUEST:	REQUEST BY:

LOCATION:	TELEPHONE:

PROBLEM:

PRIORITY URGENT ◯ NOT URGENT ◯ NOT VERY URGENT ◯

ASSIGNED TO:	DATE STARTED:	DATE COMPLETED:

TOTAL TIME SPENT:	TOTAL COST:

COMMENT:

Company's copy

REQUEST NO:	DATE OF REQUEST:	REQUEST BY:

LOCATION:	TELEPHONE:

PROBLEM:

PRIORITY URGENT ◯ NOT URGENT ◯ NOT VERY URGENT ◯

ASSIGNED TO:	DATE STARTED:	DATE COMPLETED:

TOTAL TIME SPENT:	TOTAL COST:

COMMENT:

- ✂

REQUEST NO:	DATE OF REQUEST:	REQUEST BY:

LOCATION:	TELEPHONE:

PROBLEM:

PRIORITY URGENT ◯ NOT URGENT ◯ NOT VERY URGENT ◯

ASSIGNED TO:	DATE STARTED:	DATE COMPLETED:

TOTAL TIME SPENT:	TOTAL COST:

COMMENT:

Company's copy

REQUEST NO:	DATE OF REQUEST:	REQUEST BY:

LOCATION:	TELEPHONE:

PROBLEM:

PRIORITY URGENT ◯ NOT URGENT ◯ NOT VERY URGENT ◯

ASSIGNED TO:	DATE STARTED:	DATE COMPLETED:

TOTAL TIME SPENT:	TOTAL COST:

COMMENT:

- ✂

REQUEST NO:	DATE OF REQUEST:	REQUEST BY:

LOCATION:	TELEPHONE:

PROBLEM:

PRIORITY URGENT ◯ NOT URGENT ◯ NOT VERY URGENT ◯

ASSIGNED TO:	DATE STARTED:	DATE COMPLETED:

TOTAL TIME SPENT:	TOTAL COST:

COMMENT:

Company's copy

REQUEST NO:	DATE OF REQUEST:	REQUEST BY:

LOCATION:	TELEPHONE:

PROBLEM:

PRIORITY   URGENT ◯   NOT URGENT ◯   NOT VERY URGENT ◯

ASSIGNED TO:	DATE STARTED:	DATE COMPLETED:

TOTAL TIME SPENT:	TOTAL COST:

COMMENT:

- ✂

REQUEST NO:	DATE OF REQUEST:	REQUEST BY:

LOCATION:	TELEPHONE:

PROBLEM:

PRIORITY   URGENT ◯   NOT URGENT ◯   NOT VERY URGENT ◯

ASSIGNED TO:	DATE STARTED:	DATE COMPLETED:

TOTAL TIME SPENT:	TOTAL COST:

COMMENT:

Company's copy

REQUEST NO:	DATE OF REQUEST:	REQUEST BY:

LOCATION:	TELEPHONE:

PROBLEM:

PRIORITY   URGENT ◯   NOT URGENT ◯   NOT VERY URGENT ◯

ASSIGNED TO:	DATE STARTED:	DATE COMPLETED:

TOTAL TIME SPENT:	TOTAL COST:

COMMENT:

- ✂

REQUEST NO:	DATE OF REQUEST:	REQUEST BY:

LOCATION:	TELEPHONE:

PROBLEM:

PRIORITY   URGENT ◯   NOT URGENT ◯   NOT VERY URGENT ◯

ASSIGNED TO:	DATE STARTED:	DATE COMPLETED:

TOTAL TIME SPENT:	TOTAL COST:

COMMENT:

Company's copy

REQUEST NO:	DATE OF REQUEST:	REQUEST BY:

LOCATION:	TELEPHONE:

PROBLEM:

PRIORITY URGENT ○ NOT URGENT ○ NOT VERY URGENT ○

ASSIGNED TO:	DATE STARTED:	DATE COMPLETED:

TOTAL TIME SPENT:	TOTAL COST:

COMMENT:

- ✂

REQUEST NO:	DATE OF REQUEST:	REQUEST BY:

LOCATION:	TELEPHONE:

PROBLEM:

PRIORITY URGENT ○ NOT URGENT ○ NOT VERY URGENT ○

ASSIGNED TO:	DATE STARTED:	DATE COMPLETED:

TOTAL TIME SPENT:	TOTAL COST:

COMMENT:

Company's copy

REQUEST NO:	DATE OF REQUEST:	REQUEST BY:

LOCATION:	TELEPHONE:

PROBLEM:

PRIORITY   URGENT ○   NOT URGENT ○   NOT VERY URGENT ○

ASSIGNED TO:	DATE STARTED:	DATE COMPLETED:

TOTAL TIME SPENT:	TOTAL COST:

COMMENT:

- ✂

REQUEST NO:	DATE OF REQUEST:	REQUEST BY:

LOCATION:	TELEPHONE:

PROBLEM:

PRIORITY   URGENT ○   NOT URGENT ○   NOT VERY URGENT ○

ASSIGNED TO:	DATE STARTED:	DATE COMPLETED:

TOTAL TIME SPENT:	TOTAL COST:

COMMENT:

Company's copy

REQUEST NO:	DATE OF REQUEST:	REQUEST BY:

LOCATION:	TELEPHONE:

PROBLEM:

PRIORITY URGENT ◯ NOT URGENT ◯ NOT VERY URGENT◯

ASSIGNED TO:	DATE STARTED:	DATE COMPLETED:

TOTAL TIME SPENT:	TOTAL COST:

COMMENT:

- ✂

REQUEST NO:	DATE OF REQUEST:	REQUEST BY:

LOCATION:	TELEPHONE:

PROBLEM:

PRIORITY URGENT ◯ NOT URGENT ◯ NOT VERY URGENT◯

ASSIGNED TO:	DATE STARTED:	DATE COMPLETED:

TOTAL TIME SPENT:	TOTAL COST:

COMMENT:

Company's copy

REQUEST NO:	DATE OF REQUEST:	REQUEST BY:

LOCATION:	TELEPHONE:

PROBLEM:

PRIORITY URGENT ○ NOT URGENT ○ NOT VERY URGENT ○

ASSIGNED TO:	DATE STARTED:	DATE COMPLETED:

TOTAL TIME SPENT:	TOTAL COST:

COMMENT:

- ✂

REQUEST NO:	DATE OF REQUEST:	REQUEST BY:

LOCATION:	TELEPHONE:

PROBLEM:

PRIORITY URGENT ○ NOT URGENT ○ NOT VERY URGENT ○

ASSIGNED TO:	DATE STARTED:	DATE COMPLETED:

TOTAL TIME SPENT:	TOTAL COST:

COMMENT:

Company's copy

REQUEST NO:	DATE OF REQUEST:	REQUEST BY:

LOCATION:	TELEPHONE:

PROBLEM:

PRIORITY   URGENT ◯   NOT URGENT ◯   NOT VERY URGENT◯

ASSIGNED TO:	DATE STARTED:	DATE COMPLETED:

TOTAL TIME SPENT:	TOTAL COST:

COMMENT:

✂ -

REQUEST NO:	DATE OF REQUEST:	REQUEST BY:

LOCATION:	TELEPHONE:

PROBLEM:

PRIORITY   URGENT ◯   NOT URGENT ◯   NOT VERY URGENT◯

ASSIGNED TO:	DATE STARTED:	DATE COMPLETED:

TOTAL TIME SPENT:	TOTAL COST:

COMMENT:

Company's copy

REQUEST NO:	DATE OF REQUEST:	REQUEST BY:

LOCATION:	TELEPHONE:

PROBLEM:

PRIORITY URGENT ◯ NOT URGENT ◯ NOT VERY URGENT ◯

ASSIGNED TO:	DATE STARTED:	DATE COMPLETED:

TOTAL TIME SPENT:	TOTAL COST:

COMMENT:

- ✂

REQUEST NO:	DATE OF REQUEST:	REQUEST BY:

LOCATION:	TELEPHONE:

PROBLEM:

PRIORITY URGENT ◯ NOT URGENT ◯ NOT VERY URGENT ◯

ASSIGNED TO:	DATE STARTED:	DATE COMPLETED:

TOTAL TIME SPENT:	TOTAL COST:

COMMENT:

Company's copy

REQUEST NO:	DATE OF REQUEST:	REQUEST BY:

LOCATION:	TELEPHONE:

PROBLEM:

PRIORITY URGENT ● NOT URGENT ● NOT VERY URGENT ●

ASSIGNED TO:	DATE STARTED:	DATE COMPLETED:

TOTAL TIME SPENT:	TOTAL COST:

COMMENT:

- ✂

REQUEST NO:	DATE OF REQUEST:	REQUEST BY:

LOCATION:	TELEPHONE:

PROBLEM:

PRIORITY URGENT ● NOT URGENT ● NOT VERY URGENT ●

ASSIGNED TO:	DATE STARTED:	DATE COMPLETED:

TOTAL TIME SPENT:	TOTAL COST:

COMMENT:

Company's copy

REQUEST NO:	DATE OF REQUEST:	REQUEST BY:

LOCATION:	TELEPHONE:

PROBLEM:

PRIORITY URGENT ◯ NOT URGENT ◯ NOT VERY URGENT ◯

ASSIGNED TO:	DATE STARTED:	DATE COMPLETED:

TOTAL TIME SPENT:	TOTAL COST:

COMMENT:

- ✂

REQUEST NO:	DATE OF REQUEST:	REQUEST BY:

LOCATION:	TELEPHONE:

PROBLEM:

PRIORITY URGENT ◯ NOT URGENT ◯ NOT VERY URGENT ◯

ASSIGNED TO:	DATE STARTED:	DATE COMPLETED:

TOTAL TIME SPENT:	TOTAL COST:

COMMENT:

Company's copy

REQUEST NO:	DATE OF REQUEST:	REQUEST BY:

LOCATION:	TELEPHONE:

PROBLEM:

PRIORITY   URGENT ⬤   NOT URGENT ⬤   NOT VERY URGENT⬤

ASSIGNED TO:	DATE STARTED:	DATE COMPLETED:

TOTAL TIME SPENT:	TOTAL COST:

COMMENT:

✂ -

REQUEST NO:	DATE OF REQUEST:	REQUEST BY:

LOCATION:	TELEPHONE:

PROBLEM:

PRIORITY   URGENT ⬤   NOT URGENT ⬤   NOT VERY URGENT⬤

ASSIGNED TO:	DATE STARTED:	DATE COMPLETED:

TOTAL TIME SPENT:	TOTAL COST:

COMMENT:

Company's copy

REQUEST NO:	DATE OF REQUEST:	REQUEST BY:

LOCATION:	TELEPHONE:

PROBLEM:

PRIORITY URGENT ◯ NOT URGENT ◯ NOT VERY URGENT ◯

ASSIGNED TO:	DATE STARTED:	DATE COMPLETED:

TOTAL TIME SPENT:	TOTAL COST:

COMMENT:

- ✂

REQUEST NO:	DATE OF REQUEST:	REQUEST BY:

LOCATION:	TELEPHONE:

PROBLEM:

PRIORITY URGENT ◯ NOT URGENT ◯ NOT VERY URGENT ◯

ASSIGNED TO:	DATE STARTED:	DATE COMPLETED:

TOTAL TIME SPENT:	TOTAL COST:

COMMENT:

Company's copy

REQUEST NO:	DATE OF REQUEST:	REQUEST BY:

LOCATION:	TELEPHONE:

PROBLEM:

PRIORITY URGENT ◯ NOT URGENT ◯ NOT VERY URGENT ◯

ASSIGNED TO:	DATE STARTED:	DATE COMPLETED:

TOTAL TIME SPENT:	TOTAL COST:

COMMENT:

- ✂

REQUEST NO:	DATE OF REQUEST:	REQUEST BY:

LOCATION:	TELEPHONE:

PROBLEM:

PRIORITY URGENT ◯ NOT URGENT ◯ NOT VERY URGENT ◯

ASSIGNED TO:	DATE STARTED:	DATE COMPLETED:

TOTAL TIME SPENT:	TOTAL COST:

COMMENT:

Company's copy

REQUEST NO:	DATE OF REQUEST:	REQUEST BY:

LOCATION:	TELEPHONE:

PROBLEM:

PRIORITY URGENT ○ NOT URGENT ○ NOT VERY URGENT ○

ASSIGNED TO:	DATE STARTED:	DATE COMPLETED:

TOTAL TIME SPENT:	TOTAL COST:

COMMENT:

- ✂

REQUEST NO:	DATE OF REQUEST:	REQUEST BY:

LOCATION:	TELEPHONE:

PROBLEM:

PRIORITY URGENT ○ NOT URGENT ○ NOT VERY URGENT ○

ASSIGNED TO:	DATE STARTED:	DATE COMPLETED:

TOTAL TIME SPENT:	TOTAL COST:

COMMENT:

Company's copy

REQUEST NO:	DATE OF REQUEST:	REQUEST BY:

LOCATION:	TELEPHONE:

PROBLEM:

PRIORITY   URGENT ⬤   NOT URGENT ⬤   NOT VERY URGENT⬤

ASSIGNED TO:	DATE STARTED:	DATE COMPLETED:

TOTAL TIME SPENT:	TOTAL COST:

COMMENT:

- ✂

REQUEST NO:	DATE OF REQUEST:	REQUEST BY:

LOCATION:	TELEPHONE:

PROBLEM:

PRIORITY   URGENT ⬤   NOT URGENT ⬤   NOT VERY URGENT⬤

ASSIGNED TO:	DATE STARTED:	DATE COMPLETED:

TOTAL TIME SPENT:	TOTAL COST:

COMMENT:

MAINTENANCE REQUEST FORM

REQUEST NO:	DATE OF REQUEST:	REQUEST BY:

LOCATION:	TELEPHONE:

PROBLEM:

PRIORITY URGENT ⬤ NOT URGENT ⬤ NOT VERY URGENT ⬤

ASSIGNED TO:	DATE STARTED:	DATE COMPLETED:

TOTAL TIME SPENT:	TOTAL COST:

COMMENT:

- ✂

REQUEST NO:	DATE OF REQUEST:	REQUEST BY:

LOCATION:	TELEPHONE:

PROBLEM:

PRIORITY URGENT ⬤ NOT URGENT ⬤ NOT VERY URGENT ⬤

ASSIGNED TO:	DATE STARTED:	DATE COMPLETED:

TOTAL TIME SPENT:	TOTAL COST:

COMMENT:

Company's copy

REQUEST NO:	DATE OF REQUEST:	REQUEST BY:

LOCATION:	TELEPHONE:

PROBLEM:

PRIORITY URGENT ◯ NOT URGENT ◯ NOT VERY URGENT ◯

ASSIGNED TO:	DATE STARTED:	DATE COMPLETED:

TOTAL TIME SPENT:	TOTAL COST:

COMMENT:

- ✂

REQUEST NO:	DATE OF REQUEST:	REQUEST BY:

LOCATION:	TELEPHONE:

PROBLEM:

PRIORITY URGENT ◯ NOT URGENT ◯ NOT VERY URGENT ◯

ASSIGNED TO:	DATE STARTED:	DATE COMPLETED:

TOTAL TIME SPENT:	TOTAL COST:

COMMENT:

Company's copy

REQUEST NO:	DATE OF REQUEST:	REQUEST BY:

LOCATION:	TELEPHONE:

PROBLEM:

PRIORITY URGENT ◯ NOT URGENT ◯ NOT VERY URGENT◯

ASSIGNED TO:	DATE STARTED:	DATE COMPLETED:

TOTAL TIME SPENT:	TOTAL COST:

COMMENT:

- ✂

REQUEST NO:	DATE OF REQUEST:	REQUEST BY:

LOCATION:	TELEPHONE:

PROBLEM:

PRIORITY URGENT ◯ NOT URGENT ◯ NOT VERY URGENT◯

ASSIGNED TO:	DATE STARTED:	DATE COMPLETED:

TOTAL TIME SPENT:	TOTAL COST:

COMMENT:

95

Company's copy

REQUEST NO:	DATE OF REQUEST:	REQUEST BY:

LOCATION:	TELEPHONE:

PROBLEM:

PRIORITY URGENT ⬤ NOT URGENT ⬤ NOT VERY URGENT ⬤

ASSIGNED TO:	DATE STARTED:	DATE COMPLETED:

TOTAL TIME SPENT:	TOTAL COST:

COMMENT:

- ✂

REQUEST NO:	DATE OF REQUEST:	REQUEST BY:

LOCATION:	TELEPHONE:

PROBLEM:

PRIORITY URGENT ⬤ NOT URGENT ⬤ NOT VERY URGENT ⬤

ASSIGNED TO:	DATE STARTED:	DATE COMPLETED:

TOTAL TIME SPENT:	TOTAL COST:

COMMENT:

Company's copy

REQUEST NO:	DATE OF REQUEST:	REQUEST BY:

LOCATION:	TELEPHONE:

PROBLEM:

PRIORITY URGENT ◯ NOT URGENT ◯ NOT VERY URGENT ◯

ASSIGNED TO:	DATE STARTED:	DATE COMPLETED:

TOTAL TIME SPENT:	TOTAL COST:

COMMENT:

- ✂

REQUEST NO:	DATE OF REQUEST:	REQUEST BY:

LOCATION:	TELEPHONE:

PROBLEM:

PRIORITY URGENT ◯ NOT URGENT ◯ NOT VERY URGENT ◯

ASSIGNED TO:	DATE STARTED:	DATE COMPLETED:

TOTAL TIME SPENT:	TOTAL COST:

COMMENT:

Company's copy

REQUEST NO:	DATE OF REQUEST:	REQUEST BY:

LOCATION:	TELEPHONE:

PROBLEM:

PRIORITY URGENT ◯ NOT URGENT ◯ NOT VERY URGENT ◯

ASSIGNED TO:	DATE STARTED:	DATE COMPLETED:

TOTAL TIME SPENT:	TOTAL COST:

COMMENT:

- ✂

REQUEST NO:	DATE OF REQUEST:	REQUEST BY:

LOCATION:	TELEPHONE:

PROBLEM:

PRIORITY URGENT ◯ NOT URGENT ◯ NOT VERY URGENT ◯

ASSIGNED TO:	DATE STARTED:	DATE COMPLETED:

TOTAL TIME SPENT:	TOTAL COST:

COMMENT:

Company's copy

REQUEST NO:	DATE OF REQUEST:	REQUEST BY:

LOCATION:	TELEPHONE:

PROBLEM:

PRIORITY URGENT ◯ NOT URGENT ◯ NOT VERY URGENT ◯

ASSIGNED TO:	DATE STARTED:	DATE COMPLETED:

TOTAL TIME SPENT:	TOTAL COST:

COMMENT:

- ✂

REQUEST NO:	DATE OF REQUEST:	REQUEST BY:

LOCATION:	TELEPHONE:

PROBLEM:

PRIORITY URGENT ◯ NOT URGENT ◯ NOT VERY URGENT ◯

ASSIGNED TO:	DATE STARTED:	DATE COMPLETED:

TOTAL TIME SPENT:	TOTAL COST:

COMMENT:

Company's copy

REQUEST NO:	DATE OF REQUEST:	REQUEST BY:

LOCATION:	TELEPHONE:

PROBLEM:

PRIORITY   URGENT ◯   NOT URGENT ◯   NOT VERY URGENT ◯

ASSIGNED TO:	DATE STARTED:	DATE COMPLETED:

TOTAL TIME SPENT:	TOTAL COST:

COMMENT:

- ✂

REQUEST NO:	DATE OF REQUEST:	REQUEST BY:

LOCATION:	TELEPHONE:

PROBLEM:

PRIORITY   URGENT ◯   NOT URGENT ◯   NOT VERY URGENT ◯

ASSIGNED TO:	DATE STARTED:	DATE COMPLETED:

TOTAL TIME SPENT:	TOTAL COST:

COMMENT:

Company's copy

REQUEST NO:	DATE OF REQUEST:	REQUEST BY:

LOCATION:	TELEPHONE:

PROBLEM:

PRIORITY URGENT ◯ NOT URGENT ◯ NOT VERY URGENT ◯

ASSIGNED TO:	DATE STARTED:	DATE COMPLETED:

TOTAL TIME SPENT:	TOTAL COST:

COMMENT:

- ✂

REQUEST NO:	DATE OF REQUEST:	REQUEST BY:

LOCATION:	TELEPHONE:

PROBLEM:

PRIORITY URGENT ◯ NOT URGENT ◯ NOT VERY URGENT ◯

ASSIGNED TO:	DATE STARTED:	DATE COMPLETED:

TOTAL TIME SPENT:	TOTAL COST:

COMMENT:

Company's copy

REQUEST NO:	DATE OF REQUEST:	REQUEST BY:

LOCATION:	TELEPHONE:

PROBLEM:

PRIORITY   URGENT ◯   NOT URGENT ◯   NOT VERY URGENT ◯

ASSIGNED TO:	DATE STARTED:	DATE COMPLETED:

TOTAL TIME SPENT:	TOTAL COST:

COMMENT:

- ✂

REQUEST NO:	DATE OF REQUEST:	REQUEST BY:

LOCATION:	TELEPHONE:

PROBLEM:

PRIORITY   URGENT ◯   NOT URGENT ◯   NOT VERY URGENT ◯

ASSIGNED TO:	DATE STARTED:	DATE COMPLETED:

TOTAL TIME SPENT:	TOTAL COST:

COMMENT:

Company's copy

REQUEST NO:	DATE OF REQUEST:	REQUEST BY:

LOCATION:	TELEPHONE:

PROBLEM:

PRIORITY URGENT ◯ NOT URGENT ◯ NOT VERY URGENT ◯

ASSIGNED TO:	DATE STARTED:	DATE COMPLETED:

TOTAL TIME SPENT:	TOTAL COST:

COMMENT:

----- ✂ -----

REQUEST NO:	DATE OF REQUEST:	REQUEST BY:

LOCATION:	TELEPHONE:

PROBLEM:

PRIORITY URGENT ◯ NOT URGENT ◯ NOT VERY URGENT ◯

ASSIGNED TO:	DATE STARTED:	DATE COMPLETED:

TOTAL TIME SPENT:	TOTAL COST:

COMMENT:

Company's copy

REQUEST NO:	DATE OF REQUEST:	REQUEST BY:

LOCATION:	TELEPHONE:

PROBLEM:

PRIORITY URGENT ⚪ NOT URGENT ⚪ NOT VERY URGENT ⚪

ASSIGNED TO:	DATE STARTED:	DATE COMPLETED:

TOTAL TIME SPENT:	TOTAL COST:

COMMENT:

---- ✂ ----

REQUEST NO:	DATE OF REQUEST:	REQUEST BY:

LOCATION:	TELEPHONE:

PROBLEM:

PRIORITY URGENT ⚪ NOT URGENT ⚪ NOT VERY URGENT ⚪

ASSIGNED TO:	DATE STARTED:	DATE COMPLETED:

TOTAL TIME SPENT:	TOTAL COST:

COMMENT:

MAINTENANCE REQUEST FORM

REQUEST NO:	DATE OF REQUEST:	REQUEST BY:

LOCATION:	TELEPHONE:

PROBLEM:

PRIORITY URGENT ○ NOT URGENT ○ NOT VERY URGENT ○

ASSIGNED TO:	DATE STARTED:	DATE COMPLETED:

TOTAL TIME SPENT:	TOTAL COST:

COMMENT:

- ✂

REQUEST NO:	DATE OF REQUEST:	REQUEST BY:

LOCATION:	TELEPHONE:

PROBLEM:

PRIORITY URGENT ○ NOT URGENT ○ NOT VERY URGENT ○

ASSIGNED TO:	DATE STARTED:	DATE COMPLETED:

TOTAL TIME SPENT:	TOTAL COST:

COMMENT:

Company's copy

REQUEST NO:	DATE OF REQUEST:	REQUEST BY:

LOCATION:	TELEPHONE:

PROBLEM:

PRIORITY URGENT ◯ NOT URGENT ◯ NOT VERY URGENT ◯

ASSIGNED TO:	DATE STARTED:	DATE COMPLETED:

TOTAL TIME SPENT:	TOTAL COST:

COMMENT:

- ✂

REQUEST NO:	DATE OF REQUEST:	REQUEST BY:

LOCATION:	TELEPHONE:

PROBLEM:

PRIORITY URGENT ◯ NOT URGENT ◯ NOT VERY URGENT ◯

ASSIGNED TO:	DATE STARTED:	DATE COMPLETED:

TOTAL TIME SPENT:	TOTAL COST:

COMMENT:

MAINTENANCE REQUEST FORM

REQUEST NO:	DATE OF REQUEST:	REQUEST BY:

LOCATION:	TELEPHONE:

PROBLEM:

PRIORITY   URGENT ◯   NOT URGENT ◯   NOT VERY URGENT ◯

ASSIGNED TO:	DATE STARTED:	DATE COMPLETED:

TOTAL TIME SPENT:	TOTAL COST:

COMMENT:

- ✂

REQUEST NO:	DATE OF REQUEST:	REQUEST BY:

LOCATION:	TELEPHONE:

PROBLEM:

PRIORITY   URGENT ◯   NOT URGENT ◯   NOT VERY URGENT ◯

ASSIGNED TO:	DATE STARTED:	DATE COMPLETED:

TOTAL TIME SPENT:	TOTAL COST:

COMMENT:

Company's copy

REQUEST NO:	DATE OF REQUEST:	REQUEST BY:

LOCATION:	TELEPHONE:

PROBLEM:

PRIORITY URGENT ⚪ NOT URGENT ⚪ NOT VERY URGENT ⚪

ASSIGNED TO:	DATE STARTED:	DATE COMPLETED:

TOTAL TIME SPENT:	TOTAL COST:

COMMENT:

- ✂

REQUEST NO:	DATE OF REQUEST:	REQUEST BY:

LOCATION:	TELEPHONE:

PROBLEM:

PRIORITY URGENT ⚪ NOT URGENT ⚪ NOT VERY URGENT ⚪

ASSIGNED TO:	DATE STARTED:	DATE COMPLETED:

TOTAL TIME SPENT:	TOTAL COST:

COMMENT:

121

Company's copy

REQUEST NO:	DATE OF REQUEST:	REQUEST BY:

LOCATION:	TELEPHONE:

PROBLEM:

PRIORITY URGENT ◯ NOT URGENT ◯ NOT VERY URGENT ◯

ASSIGNED TO:	DATE STARTED:	DATE COMPLETED:

TOTAL TIME SPENT:	TOTAL COST:

COMMENT:

✂ -

REQUEST NO:	DATE OF REQUEST:	REQUEST BY:

LOCATION:	TELEPHONE:

PROBLEM:

PRIORITY URGENT ◯ NOT URGENT ◯ NOT VERY URGENT ◯

ASSIGNED TO:	DATE STARTED:	DATE COMPLETED:

TOTAL TIME SPENT:	TOTAL COST:

COMMENT:

Company's copy

REQUEST NO:	DATE OF REQUEST:	REQUEST BY:

LOCATION:	TELEPHONE:

PROBLEM:

PRIORITY   URGENT ⬤   NOT URGENT ⬤   NOT VERY URGENT ⬤

ASSIGNED TO:	DATE STARTED:	DATE COMPLETED:

TOTAL TIME SPENT:	TOTAL COST:

COMMENT:

- ✂

REQUEST NO:	DATE OF REQUEST:	REQUEST BY:

LOCATION:	TELEPHONE:

PROBLEM:

PRIORITY   URGENT ⬤   NOT URGENT ⬤   NOT VERY URGENT ⬤

ASSIGNED TO:	DATE STARTED:	DATE COMPLETED:

TOTAL TIME SPENT:	TOTAL COST:

COMMENT:

Company's copy

REQUEST NO:	DATE OF REQUEST:	REQUEST BY:

LOCATION:	TELEPHONE:

PROBLEM:

PRIORITY URGENT ◯ NOT URGENT ◯ NOT VERY URGENT ◯

ASSIGNED TO:	DATE STARTED:	DATE COMPLETED:

TOTAL TIME SPENT:	TOTAL COST:

COMMENT:

✂ ···

REQUEST NO:	DATE OF REQUEST:	REQUEST BY:

LOCATION:	TELEPHONE:

PROBLEM:

PRIORITY URGENT ◯ NOT URGENT ◯ NOT VERY URGENT ◯

ASSIGNED TO:	DATE STARTED:	DATE COMPLETED:

TOTAL TIME SPENT:	TOTAL COST:

COMMENT:

127

Company's copy

REQUEST NO:	DATE OF REQUEST:	REQUEST BY:

LOCATION:		TELEPHONE:

PROBLEM:

PRIORITY   URGENT ◯   NOT URGENT ◯   NOT VERY URGENT ◯

ASSIGNED TO:	DATE STARTED:	DATE COMPLETED:

TOTAL TIME SPENT:	TOTAL COST:

COMMENT:

✂ ┈┈┈┈┈┈┈┈┈┈┈┈┈┈┈┈┈┈┈┈┈┈┈┈┈┈┈┈┈┈┈┈┈┈┈┈┈┈

REQUEST NO:	DATE OF REQUEST:	REQUEST BY:

LOCATION:		TELEPHONE:

PROBLEM:

PRIORITY   URGENT ◯   NOT URGENT ◯   NOT VERY URGENT ◯

ASSIGNED TO:	DATE STARTED:	DATE COMPLETED:

TOTAL TIME SPENT:	TOTAL COST:

COMMENT:

MAINTENANCE REQUEST FORM

REQUEST NO:	DATE OF REQUEST:	REQUEST BY:

LOCATION:	TELEPHONE:

PROBLEM:

PRIORITY URGENT ◯ NOT URGENT ◯ NOT VERY URGENT ◯

ASSIGNED TO:	DATE STARTED:	DATE COMPLETED:

TOTAL TIME SPENT:	TOTAL COST:

COMMENT:

- ✂

REQUEST NO:	DATE OF REQUEST:	REQUEST BY:

LOCATION:	TELEPHONE:

PROBLEM:

PRIORITY URGENT ◯ NOT URGENT ◯ NOT VERY URGENT ◯

ASSIGNED TO:	DATE STARTED:	DATE COMPLETED:

TOTAL TIME SPENT:	TOTAL COST:

COMMENT:

Company's copy

REQUEST NO:	DATE OF REQUEST:	REQUEST BY:

LOCATION:	TELEPHONE:

PROBLEM:

PRIORITY   URGENT ◯   NOT URGENT ◯   NOT VERY URGENT ◯

ASSIGNED TO:	DATE STARTED:	DATE COMPLETED:

TOTAL TIME SPENT:	TOTAL COST:

COMMENT:

-- ✂

REQUEST NO:	DATE OF REQUEST:	REQUEST BY:

LOCATION:	TELEPHONE:

PROBLEM:

PRIORITY   URGENT ◯   NOT URGENT ◯   NOT VERY URGENT ◯

ASSIGNED TO:	DATE STARTED:	DATE COMPLETED:

TOTAL TIME SPENT:	TOTAL COST:

COMMENT:

Company's copy

REQUEST NO:	DATE OF REQUEST:	REQUEST BY:

LOCATION:	TELEPHONE:

PROBLEM:

PRIORITY　URGENT ◯　NOT URGENT ◯　NOT VERY URGENT ◯

ASSIGNED TO:	DATE STARTED:	DATE COMPLETED:

TOTAL TIME SPENT:	TOTAL COST:

COMMENT:

- ✂

REQUEST NO:	DATE OF REQUEST:	REQUEST BY:

LOCATION:	TELEPHONE:

PROBLEM:

PRIORITY　URGENT ◯　NOT URGENT ◯　NOT VERY URGENT ◯

ASSIGNED TO:	DATE STARTED:	DATE COMPLETED:

TOTAL TIME SPENT:	TOTAL COST:

COMMENT:

Company's copy

REQUEST NO:	DATE OF REQUEST:	REQUEST BY:

LOCATION:	TELEPHONE:

PROBLEM:

PRIORITY   URGENT ◯   NOT URGENT ◯   NOT VERY URGENT ◯

ASSIGNED TO:	DATE STARTED:	DATE COMPLETED:

TOTAL TIME SPENT:	TOTAL COST:

COMMENT:

- ✂

REQUEST NO:	DATE OF REQUEST:	REQUEST BY:

LOCATION:	TELEPHONE:

PROBLEM:

PRIORITY   URGENT ◯   NOT URGENT ◯   NOT VERY URGENT ◯

ASSIGNED TO:	DATE STARTED:	DATE COMPLETED:

TOTAL TIME SPENT:	TOTAL COST:

COMMENT:

Company's copy

REQUEST NO:	DATE OF REQUEST:	REQUEST BY:

LOCATION:	TELEPHONE:

PROBLEM:

PRIORITY   URGENT ◯   NOT URGENT ◯   NOT VERY URGENT ◯

ASSIGNED TO:	DATE STARTED:	DATE COMPLETED:

TOTAL TIME SPENT:	TOTAL COST:

COMMENT:

- ✂

REQUEST NO:	DATE OF REQUEST:	REQUEST BY:

LOCATION:	TELEPHONE:

PROBLEM:

PRIORITY   URGENT ◯   NOT URGENT ◯   NOT VERY URGENT ◯

ASSIGNED TO:	DATE STARTED:	DATE COMPLETED:

TOTAL TIME SPENT:	TOTAL COST:

COMMENT:

Company's copy

REQUEST NO:	DATE OF REQUEST:	REQUEST BY:

LOCATION:	TELEPHONE:

PROBLEM:

PRIORITY URGENT ◯ NOT URGENT ◯ NOT VERY URGENT ◯

ASSIGNED TO:	DATE STARTED:	DATE COMPLETED:

TOTAL TIME SPENT:	TOTAL COST:

COMMENT:

✂ ┈┈

REQUEST NO:	DATE OF REQUEST:	REQUEST BY:

LOCATION:	TELEPHONE:

PROBLEM:

PRIORITY URGENT ◯ NOT URGENT ◯ NOT VERY URGENT ◯

ASSIGNED TO:	DATE STARTED:	DATE COMPLETED:

TOTAL TIME SPENT:	TOTAL COST:

COMMENT:

Company's copy

REQUEST NO:	DATE OF REQUEST:	REQUEST BY:

LOCATION:	TELEPHONE:

PROBLEM:

PRIORITY URGENT ◯ NOT URGENT ◯ NOT VERY URGENT ◯

ASSIGNED TO:	DATE STARTED:	DATE COMPLETED:

TOTAL TIME SPENT:	TOTAL COST:

COMMENT:

- ✂

REQUEST NO:	DATE OF REQUEST:	REQUEST BY:

LOCATION:	TELEPHONE:

PROBLEM:

PRIORITY URGENT ◯ NOT URGENT ◯ NOT VERY URGENT ◯

ASSIGNED TO:	DATE STARTED:	DATE COMPLETED:

TOTAL TIME SPENT:	TOTAL COST:

COMMENT:

Company's copy

REQUEST NO:	DATE OF REQUEST:	REQUEST BY:

LOCATION:	TELEPHONE:

PROBLEM:

PRIORITY URGENT ◯ NOT URGENT ◯ NOT VERY URGENT ◯

ASSIGNED TO:	DATE STARTED:	DATE COMPLETED:

TOTAL TIME SPENT:	TOTAL COST:

COMMENT:

- ✂

REQUEST NO:	DATE OF REQUEST:	REQUEST BY:

LOCATION:	TELEPHONE:

PROBLEM:

PRIORITY URGENT ◯ NOT URGENT ◯ NOT VERY URGENT ◯

ASSIGNED TO:	DATE STARTED:	DATE COMPLETED:

TOTAL TIME SPENT:	TOTAL COST:

COMMENT:

Company's copy

REQUEST NO:	DATE OF REQUEST:	REQUEST BY:	

LOCATION:		TELEPHONE:

PROBLEM:

PRIORITY URGENT ◯ NOT URGENT ◯ NOT VERY URGENT ◯

ASSIGNED TO:	DATE STARTED:	DATE COMPLETED:

TOTAL TIME SPENT:	TOTAL COST:

COMMENT:

- ✂

REQUEST NO:	DATE OF REQUEST:	REQUEST BY:	

LOCATION:		TELEPHONE:

PROBLEM:

PRIORITY URGENT ◯ NOT URGENT ◯ NOT VERY URGENT ◯

ASSIGNED TO:	DATE STARTED:	DATE COMPLETED:

TOTAL TIME SPENT:	TOTAL COST:

COMMENT:

Company's copy

REQUEST NO:	DATE OF REQUEST:	REQUEST BY:

LOCATION:	TELEPHONE:

PROBLEM:

PRIORITY URGENT ◯ NOT URGENT ◯ NOT VERY URGENT ◯

ASSIGNED TO:	DATE STARTED:	DATE COMPLETED:

TOTAL TIME SPENT:	TOTAL COST:

COMMENT:

- ✂

REQUEST NO:	DATE OF REQUEST:	REQUEST BY:

LOCATION:	TELEPHONE:

PROBLEM:

PRIORITY URGENT ◯ NOT URGENT ◯ NOT VERY URGENT ◯

ASSIGNED TO:	DATE STARTED:	DATE COMPLETED:

TOTAL TIME SPENT:	TOTAL COST:

COMMENT:

Company's copy

REQUEST NO:	DATE OF REQUEST:	REQUEST BY:

LOCATION:	TELEPHONE:

PROBLEM:

PRIORITY   URGENT ◯   NOT URGENT ◯   NOT VERY URGENT ◯

ASSIGNED TO:	DATE STARTED:	DATE COMPLETED:

TOTAL TIME SPENT:	TOTAL COST:

COMMENT:

- ✂

REQUEST NO:	DATE OF REQUEST:	REQUEST BY:

LOCATION:	TELEPHONE:

PROBLEM:

PRIORITY   URGENT ◯   NOT URGENT ◯   NOT VERY URGENT ◯

ASSIGNED TO:	DATE STARTED:	DATE COMPLETED:

TOTAL TIME SPENT:	TOTAL COST:

COMMENT:

Company's copy

REQUEST NO:	DATE OF REQUEST:	REQUEST BY:

LOCATION:	TELEPHONE:

PROBLEM:

PRIORITY   URGENT ◯   NOT URGENT ◯   NOT VERY URGENT ◯

ASSIGNED TO:	DATE STARTED:	DATE COMPLETED:

TOTAL TIME SPENT:	TOTAL COST:

COMMENT:

- ✂

REQUEST NO:	DATE OF REQUEST:	REQUEST BY:

LOCATION:	TELEPHONE:

PROBLEM:

PRIORITY   URGENT ◯   NOT URGENT ◯   NOT VERY URGENT ◯

ASSIGNED TO:	DATE STARTED:	DATE COMPLETED:

TOTAL TIME SPENT:	TOTAL COST:

COMMENT:

Company's copy

REQUEST NO:	DATE OF REQUEST:	REQUEST BY:

LOCATION:		TELEPHONE:

PROBLEM:

PRIORITY   URGENT ◯   NOT URGENT ◯   NOT VERY URGENT ◯

ASSIGNED TO:	DATE STARTED:	DATE COMPLETED:

TOTAL TIME SPENT:	TOTAL COST:

COMMENT:

- ✄

REQUEST NO:	DATE OF REQUEST:	REQUEST BY:

LOCATION:		TELEPHONE:

PROBLEM:

PRIORITY   URGENT ◯   NOT URGENT ◯   NOT VERY URGENT ◯

ASSIGNED TO:	DATE STARTED:	DATE COMPLETED:

TOTAL TIME SPENT:	TOTAL COST:

COMMENT:

Company's copy

REQUEST NO:	DATE OF REQUEST:	REQUEST BY:

LOCATION:	TELEPHONE:

PROBLEM:

PRIORITY URGENT ◯ NOT URGENT ◯ NOT VERY URGENT ◯

ASSIGNED TO:	DATE STARTED:	DATE COMPLETED:

TOTAL TIME SPENT:	TOTAL COST:

COMMENT:

- ✂

REQUEST NO:	DATE OF REQUEST:	REQUEST BY:

LOCATION:	TELEPHONE:

PROBLEM:

PRIORITY URGENT ◯ NOT URGENT ◯ NOT VERY URGENT ◯

ASSIGNED TO:	DATE STARTED:	DATE COMPLETED:

TOTAL TIME SPENT:	TOTAL COST:

COMMENT:

MAINTENANCE REQUEST FORM

REQUEST NO:	DATE OF REQUEST:	REQUEST BY:

LOCATION:	TELEPHONE:

PROBLEM:

PRIORITY   URGENT ○   NOT URGENT ○   NOT VERY URGENT ○

ASSIGNED TO:	DATE STARTED:	DATE COMPLETED:

TOTAL TIME SPENT:	TOTAL COST:

COMMENT:

- ✂

REQUEST NO:	DATE OF REQUEST:	REQUEST BY:

LOCATION:	TELEPHONE:

PROBLEM:

PRIORITY   URGENT ○   NOT URGENT ○   NOT VERY URGENT ○

ASSIGNED TO:	DATE STARTED:	DATE COMPLETED:

TOTAL TIME SPENT:	TOTAL COST:

COMMENT:

MAINTENANCE REQUEST FORM

REQUEST NO:	DATE OF REQUEST:	REQUEST BY:

LOCATION:	TELEPHONE:

PROBLEM:

PRIORITY   URGENT ◯   NOT URGENT ◯   NOT VERY URGENT ◯

ASSIGNED TO:	DATE STARTED:	DATE COMPLETED:

TOTAL TIME SPENT:	TOTAL COST:

COMMENT:

------------------------------✄

REQUEST NO:	DATE OF REQUEST:	REQUEST BY:

LOCATION:	TELEPHONE:

PROBLEM:

PRIORITY   URGENT ◯   NOT URGENT ◯   NOT VERY URGENT ◯

ASSIGNED TO:	DATE STARTED:	DATE COMPLETED:

TOTAL TIME SPENT:	TOTAL COST:

COMMENT:

Company's copy

REQUEST NO:	DATE OF REQUEST:	REQUEST BY:

LOCATION:	TELEPHONE:

PROBLEM:

PRIORITY URGENT ⬤ NOT URGENT ⬤ NOT VERY URGENT ⬤

ASSIGNED TO:	DATE STARTED:	DATE COMPLETED:

TOTAL TIME SPENT:	TOTAL COST:

COMMENT:

✂ -

REQUEST NO:	DATE OF REQUEST:	REQUEST BY:

LOCATION:	TELEPHONE:

PROBLEM:

PRIORITY URGENT ⬤ NOT URGENT ⬤ NOT VERY URGENT ⬤

ASSIGNED TO:	DATE STARTED:	DATE COMPLETED:

TOTAL TIME SPENT:	TOTAL COST:

COMMENT:

MAINTENANCE REQUEST FORM

REQUEST NO:	DATE OF REQUEST:	REQUEST BY:

LOCATION:	TELEPHONE:

PROBLEM:

PRIORITY   URGENT ◯   NOT URGENT ◯   NOT VERY URGENT ◯

ASSIGNED TO:	DATE STARTED:	DATE COMPLETED:

TOTAL TIME SPENT:	TOTAL COST:

COMMENT:

✂ ···

REQUEST NO:	DATE OF REQUEST:	REQUEST BY:

LOCATION:	TELEPHONE:

PROBLEM:

PRIORITY   URGENT ◯   NOT URGENT ◯   NOT VERY URGENT ◯

ASSIGNED TO:	DATE STARTED:	DATE COMPLETED:

TOTAL TIME SPENT:	TOTAL COST:

COMMENT:

Company's copy

REQUEST NO:	DATE OF REQUEST:	REQUEST BY:

LOCATION:	TELEPHONE:

PROBLEM:

PRIORITY URGENT ⬤ NOT URGENT ⬤ NOT VERY URGENT ⬤

ASSIGNED TO:	DATE STARTED:	DATE COMPLETED:

TOTAL TIME SPENT:	TOTAL COST:

COMMENT:

- ✂

REQUEST NO:	DATE OF REQUEST:	REQUEST BY:

LOCATION:	TELEPHONE:

PROBLEM:

PRIORITY URGENT ⬤ NOT URGENT ⬤ NOT VERY URGENT ⬤

ASSIGNED TO:	DATE STARTED:	DATE COMPLETED:

TOTAL TIME SPENT:	TOTAL COST:

COMMENT:

Company's copy

REQUEST NO:	DATE OF REQUEST:	REQUEST BY:

LOCATION:	TELEPHONE:

PROBLEM:

PRIORITY URGENT ◯ NOT URGENT ◯ NOT VERY URGENT ◯

ASSIGNED TO:	DATE STARTED:	DATE COMPLETED:

TOTAL TIME SPENT:	TOTAL COST:

COMMENT:

- ✂

REQUEST NO:	DATE OF REQUEST:	REQUEST BY:

LOCATION:	TELEPHONE:

PROBLEM:

PRIORITY URGENT ◯ NOT URGENT ◯ NOT VERY URGENT ◯

ASSIGNED TO:	DATE STARTED:	DATE COMPLETED:

TOTAL TIME SPENT:	TOTAL COST:

COMMENT:

Company's copy

REQUEST NO:	DATE OF REQUEST:	REQUEST BY:

LOCATION:	TELEPHONE:

PROBLEM:

PRIORITY URGENT ◯ NOT URGENT ◯ NOT VERY URGENT ◯

ASSIGNED TO:	DATE STARTED:	DATE COMPLETED:

TOTAL TIME SPENT:	TOTAL COST:

COMMENT:

- ✂

REQUEST NO:	DATE OF REQUEST:	REQUEST BY:

LOCATION:	TELEPHONE:

PROBLEM:

PRIORITY URGENT ◯ NOT URGENT ◯ NOT VERY URGENT ◯

ASSIGNED TO:	DATE STARTED:	DATE COMPLETED:

TOTAL TIME SPENT:	TOTAL COST:

COMMENT:

Company's copy

REQUEST NO:	DATE OF REQUEST:	REQUEST BY:	
LOCATION:		TELEPHONE:	
PROBLEM:			

PRIORITY   URGENT ◯   NOT URGENT ◯   NOT VERY URGENT ◯

ASSIGNED TO:	DATE STARTED:	DATE COMPLETED:
TOTAL TIME SPENT:	TOTAL COST:	
COMMENT:		

- ✂

REQUEST NO:	DATE OF REQUEST:	REQUEST BY:	
LOCATION:		TELEPHONE:	
PROBLEM:			

PRIORITY   URGENT ◯   NOT URGENT ◯   NOT VERY URGENT ◯

ASSIGNED TO:	DATE STARTED:	DATE COMPLETED:
TOTAL TIME SPENT:	TOTAL COST:	
COMMENT:		

Company's copy

REQUEST NO:	DATE OF REQUEST:	REQUEST BY:

LOCATION:	TELEPHONE:

PROBLEM:

PRIORITY URGENT ◯ NOT URGENT ◯ NOT VERY URGENT◯

ASSIGNED TO:	DATE STARTED:	DATE COMPLETED:

TOTAL TIME SPENT:	TOTAL COST:

COMMENT:

- ✂

REQUEST NO:	DATE OF REQUEST:	REQUEST BY:

LOCATION:	TELEPHONE:

PROBLEM:

PRIORITY URGENT ◯ NOT URGENT ◯ NOT VERY URGENT◯

ASSIGNED TO:	DATE STARTED:	DATE COMPLETED:

TOTAL TIME SPENT:	TOTAL COST:

COMMENT:

Company's copy

REQUEST NO:	DATE OF REQUEST:	REQUEST BY:

LOCATION:	TELEPHONE:

PROBLEM:

PRIORITY URGENT ◯ NOT URGENT ◯ NOT VERY URGENT◯

ASSIGNED TO:	DATE STARTED:	DATE COMPLETED:

TOTAL TIME SPENT:	TOTAL COST:

COMMENT:

✂ -

REQUEST NO:	DATE OF REQUEST:	REQUEST BY:

LOCATION:	TELEPHONE:

PROBLEM:

PRIORITY URGENT ◯ NOT URGENT ◯ NOT VERY URGENT◯

ASSIGNED TO:	DATE STARTED:	DATE COMPLETED:

TOTAL TIME SPENT:	TOTAL COST:

COMMENT:

Company's copy

REQUEST NO:	DATE OF REQUEST:	REQUEST BY:

LOCATION:	TELEPHONE:

PROBLEM:

PRIORITY URGENT ⚪ NOT URGENT ⚪ NOT VERY URGENT ⚪

ASSIGNED TO:	DATE STARTED:	DATE COMPLETED:

TOTAL TIME SPENT:	TOTAL COST:

COMMENT:

✂ ....

REQUEST NO:	DATE OF REQUEST:	REQUEST BY:

LOCATION:	TELEPHONE:

PROBLEM:

PRIORITY URGENT ⚪ NOT URGENT ⚪ NOT VERY URGENT ⚪

ASSIGNED TO:	DATE STARTED:	DATE COMPLETED:

TOTAL TIME SPENT:	TOTAL COST:

COMMENT:

Company's copy

REQUEST NO:	DATE OF REQUEST:	REQUEST BY:

LOCATION:	TELEPHONE:

PROBLEM:

PRIORITY URGENT ◯ NOT URGENT ◯ NOT VERY URGENT ◯

ASSIGNED TO:	DATE STARTED:	DATE COMPLETED:

TOTAL TIME SPENT:	TOTAL COST:

COMMENT:

------------------------------- ✂

REQUEST NO:	DATE OF REQUEST:	REQUEST BY:

LOCATION:	TELEPHONE:

PROBLEM:

PRIORITY URGENT ◯ NOT URGENT ◯ NOT VERY URGENT ◯

ASSIGNED TO:	DATE STARTED:	DATE COMPLETED:

TOTAL TIME SPENT:	TOTAL COST:

COMMENT:

MAINTENANCE REQUEST FORM

REQUEST NO:	DATE OF REQUEST:	REQUEST BY:

LOCATION:	TELEPHONE:

PROBLEM:

PRIORITY   URGENT ◯   NOT URGENT ◯   NOT VERY URGENT ◯

ASSIGNED TO:	DATE STARTED:	DATE COMPLETED:

TOTAL TIME SPENT:	TOTAL COST:

COMMENT:

- ✂

REQUEST NO:	DATE OF REQUEST:	REQUEST BY:

LOCATION:	TELEPHONE:

PROBLEM:

PRIORITY   URGENT ◯   NOT URGENT ◯   NOT VERY URGENT ◯

ASSIGNED TO:	DATE STARTED:	DATE COMPLETED:

TOTAL TIME SPENT:	TOTAL COST:

COMMENT:

Company's copy

MAINTENANCE **REQUEST FORM**

REQUEST NO:	DATE OF REQUEST:	REQUEST BY:

LOCATION:	TELEPHONE:

PROBLEM:

PRIORITY URGENT ⚪ NOT URGENT ⚪ NOT VERY URGENT⚪

ASSIGNED TO:	DATE STARTED:	DATE COMPLETED:

TOTAL TIME SPENT:	TOTAL COST:

COMMENT:

- ✂

REQUEST NO:	DATE OF REQUEST:	REQUEST BY:

LOCATION:	TELEPHONE:

PROBLEM:

PRIORITY URGENT ⚪ NOT URGENT ⚪ NOT VERY URGENT⚪

ASSIGNED TO:	DATE STARTED:	DATE COMPLETED:

TOTAL TIME SPENT:	TOTAL COST:

COMMENT:

Company's copy

REQUEST NO:	DATE OF REQUEST:	REQUEST BY:

LOCATION:	TELEPHONE:

PROBLEM:

PRIORITY URGENT ⚪ NOT URGENT ⚪ NOT VERY URGENT ⚪

ASSIGNED TO:	DATE STARTED:	DATE COMPLETED:

TOTAL TIME SPENT:	TOTAL COST:

COMMENT:

- ✂

REQUEST NO:	DATE OF REQUEST:	REQUEST BY:

LOCATION:	TELEPHONE:

PROBLEM:

PRIORITY URGENT ⚪ NOT URGENT ⚪ NOT VERY URGENT ⚪

ASSIGNED TO:	DATE STARTED:	DATE COMPLETED:

TOTAL TIME SPENT:	TOTAL COST:

COMMENT:

MAINTENANCE REQUEST FORM

REQUEST NO:	DATE OF REQUEST:	REQUEST BY:

LOCATION:	TELEPHONE:

PROBLEM:

PRIORITY URGENT ◯ NOT URGENT ◯ NOT VERY URGENT ◯

ASSIGNED TO:	DATE STARTED:	DATE COMPLETED:

TOTAL TIME SPENT:	TOTAL COST:

COMMENT:

- ✂

REQUEST NO:	DATE OF REQUEST:	REQUEST BY:

LOCATION:	TELEPHONE:

PROBLEM:

PRIORITY URGENT ◯ NOT URGENT ◯ NOT VERY URGENT ◯

ASSIGNED TO:	DATE STARTED:	DATE COMPLETED:

TOTAL TIME SPENT:	TOTAL COST:

COMMENT:

Company's copy

REQUEST NO:	DATE OF REQUEST:	REQUEST BY:

LOCATION:	TELEPHONE:

PROBLEM:

PRIORITY URGENT ◯ NOT URGENT ◯ NOT VERY URGENT ◯

ASSIGNED TO:	DATE STARTED:	DATE COMPLETED:

TOTAL TIME SPENT:	TOTAL COST:

COMMENT:

- ✂

REQUEST NO:	DATE OF REQUEST:	REQUEST BY:

LOCATION:	TELEPHONE:

PROBLEM:

PRIORITY URGENT ◯ NOT URGENT ◯ NOT VERY URGENT ◯

ASSIGNED TO:	DATE STARTED:	DATE COMPLETED:

TOTAL TIME SPENT:	TOTAL COST:

COMMENT:

Company's copy

REQUEST NO:	DATE OF REQUEST:	REQUEST BY:

LOCATION:	TELEPHONE:

PROBLEM:

PRIORITY   URGENT ◯   NOT URGENT ◯   NOT VERY URGENT ◯

ASSIGNED TO:	DATE STARTED:	DATE COMPLETED:

TOTAL TIME SPENT:	TOTAL COST:

COMMENT:

- ✂

REQUEST NO:	DATE OF REQUEST:	REQUEST BY:

LOCATION:	TELEPHONE:

PROBLEM:

PRIORITY   URGENT ◯   NOT URGENT ◯   NOT VERY URGENT ◯

ASSIGNED TO:	DATE STARTED:	DATE COMPLETED:

TOTAL TIME SPENT:	TOTAL COST:

COMMENT:

Company's copy

REQUEST NO:	DATE OF REQUEST:	REQUEST BY:

LOCATION:	TELEPHONE:

PROBLEM:

PRIORITY   URGENT ⬤   NOT URGENT ⬤   NOT VERY URGENT ⬤

ASSIGNED TO:	DATE STARTED:	DATE COMPLETED:

TOTAL TIME SPENT:	TOTAL COST:

COMMENT:

- ✂

REQUEST NO:	DATE OF REQUEST:	REQUEST BY:

LOCATION:	TELEPHONE:

PROBLEM:

PRIORITY   URGENT ⬤   NOT URGENT ⬤   NOT VERY URGENT ⬤

ASSIGNED TO:	DATE STARTED:	DATE COMPLETED:

TOTAL TIME SPENT:	TOTAL COST:

COMMENT:

Company's copy

REQUEST NO:	DATE OF REQUEST:	REQUEST BY:

LOCATION:	TELEPHONE:

PROBLEM:

PRIORITY URGENT ◯ NOT URGENT ◯ NOT VERY URGENT ◯

ASSIGNED TO:	DATE STARTED:	DATE COMPLETED:

TOTAL TIME SPENT:	TOTAL COST:

COMMENT:

- ✂

REQUEST NO:	DATE OF REQUEST:	REQUEST BY:

LOCATION:	TELEPHONE:

PROBLEM:

PRIORITY URGENT ◯ NOT URGENT ◯ NOT VERY URGENT ◯

ASSIGNED TO:	DATE STARTED:	DATE COMPLETED:

TOTAL TIME SPENT:	TOTAL COST:

COMMENT:

Company's copy

REQUEST NO:	DATE OF REQUEST:	REQUEST BY:

LOCATION:	TELEPHONE:

PROBLEM:

PRIORITY URGENT ◯ NOT URGENT ◯ NOT VERY URGENT ◯

ASSIGNED TO:	DATE STARTED:	DATE COMPLETED:

TOTAL TIME SPENT:	TOTAL COST:

COMMENT:

- ✂

REQUEST NO:	DATE OF REQUEST:	REQUEST BY:

LOCATION:	TELEPHONE:

PROBLEM:

PRIORITY URGENT ◯ NOT URGENT ◯ NOT VERY URGENT ◯

ASSIGNED TO:	DATE STARTED:	DATE COMPLETED:

TOTAL TIME SPENT:	TOTAL COST:

COMMENT:

Company's copy

REQUEST NO:	DATE OF REQUEST:	REQUEST BY:

LOCATION:	TELEPHONE:

PROBLEM:

PRIORITY URGENT ◯ NOT URGENT ◯ NOT VERY URGENT ◯

ASSIGNED TO:	DATE STARTED:	DATE COMPLETED:

TOTAL TIME SPENT:	TOTAL COST:

COMMENT:

⋯⋯⋯⋯⋯⋯⋯⋯⋯⋯⋯⋯⋯⋯⋯⋯⋯⋯⋯⋯⋯⋯⋯⋯⋯⋯✂

REQUEST NO:	DATE OF REQUEST:	REQUEST BY:

LOCATION:	TELEPHONE:

PROBLEM:

PRIORITY URGENT ◯ NOT URGENT ◯ NOT VERY URGENT ◯

ASSIGNED TO:	DATE STARTED:	DATE COMPLETED:

TOTAL TIME SPENT:	TOTAL COST:

COMMENT:

Made in United States
Troutdale, OR
01/04/2024

16685987R00113